This Starfish Bay book belongs to

....

Watch Out, Snail!

Snail—crawling through the forest. Over and under, and there you appear!

STARFISH BAY
CHILDREN'S BOOKS

www.starfishbaypublishing.com

Watch Out, Snail!

Text copyright © Gay Hay 2017
Illustrations copyright © Margaret Tolland 2017
This edition © Starfish Bay Publishing 2017
First published in 2017
ISBN: 978-1-76036-032-0
Printed and bound in China by Beijing Shangtang Print & Packaging Co., Ltd
11 Tengren Road, Niulanshan Town, Shunyi District, Beijing, China

Also by Gay Hay and Margaret Tolland and published by Starfish Bay

Watch Out, Snail!

Written by **Gay Hay**

Illustrated by **Margaret Tolland**

Night slips in. The forest stirs.

Down in its depths lives Snail,
its shell as big as your fist.

The moon shines.
Berries glisten.

A shimmering trail winds
through the forest floor.

Darkness is a time for hunting.

Watch out, Snail!

Snail hunts through forest litter,
under branches and gnarly roots.

But others are out hunting, too.
A snail would be a tasty treat!

Hedgehog shuffles,
sniffing, snuffling.

Snail hides among the leaves.

Rat sneaks up, long whiskers twitching.

Snail slides into a hollow,
safe from Rat's marauding teeth.

Possum fossicks.
Sharp claws grasp and grab.

Snail slithers out of reach.

Pig stomps in,
strong tusks jabbing,
stirring up the forest floor.

Snail escapes beneath a log.

Alert now, eye stalks twitching,

Snail slides in closer,

slowly,

slowly.

A mighty worm for Snail to eat!

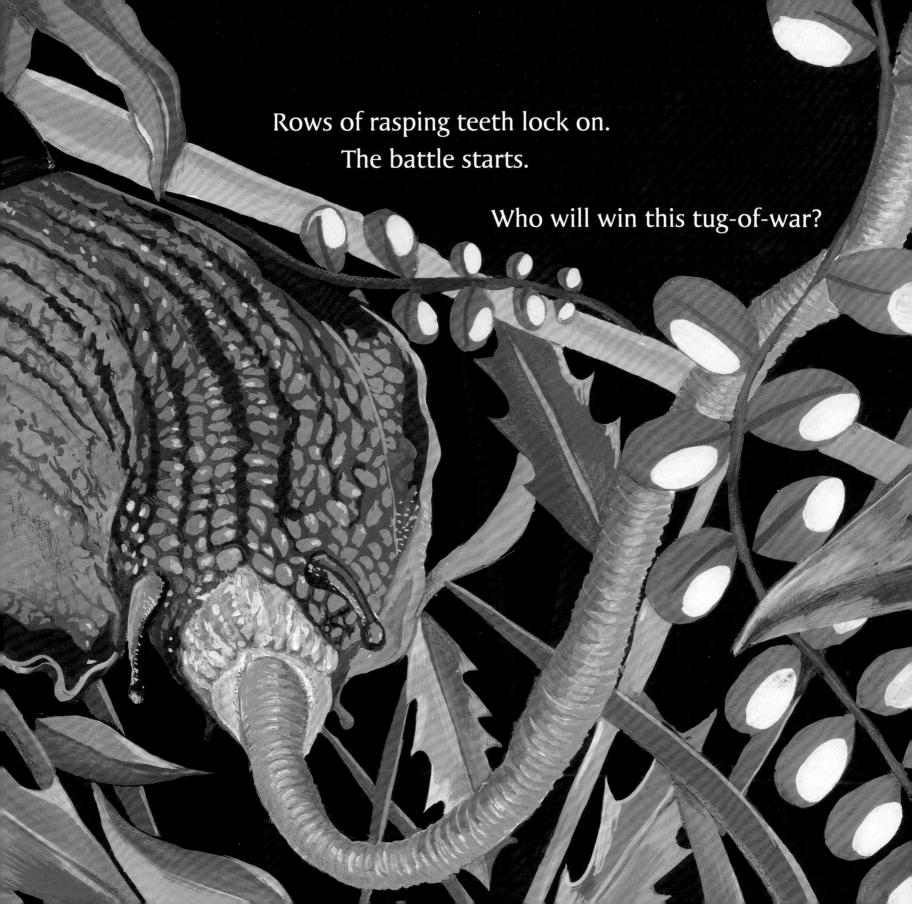

Rows of rasping teeth lock on.
The battle starts.

Who will win this tug-of-war?

A pull,

a heave,

a mighty slurp.

Snail's the winner.

Worm's the dinner.

Night is a time for hungry hunters.

Watch out!

The patterns on Powelliphanta shells always spiral clockwise.

Powelliphanta snails are carnivorous.

These are the places where Powelliphanta snails live in New Zealand.

They like to eat worms.

Weka

Powelliphanta snails have eyes on the ends of long stalks.

Snails slide along on a strong muscular foot.

Powelliphanta snails lay eggs from a slit in their neck.

Peripatus

Powelliphanta snails have thousands of teeth attached to a tongue-like structure called a radula.

When a new snail hatches, it rasps some of the calcium from its egg shell. This helps it to grow a shell of its own.

Powelliphanta snails are different from the snails we find in our garden.

Powelliphanta snails have beautiful, large, round shells. The largest ever found was 3.6 inches across. Every shell is different and has unique spiral or radial patterns in gold, brown, black, and yellow.

Powelliphanta snails live under logs and rotting leaves in damp forests. If they dry out, they will die.

They are nocturnal and come out at night to find food and to mate.

These carnivorous giants have rasping teeth. They grasp a worm with their teeth and then suck it up, just like we eat spaghetti.

Pests such as rats, pigs, possums, and hedgehogs eat Powelliphanta snails. So do birds.

Powelliphanta snails are hermaphrodites. That means that each snail is both male and female and mates with another snail just like it.

They lay 5–10 eggs a year. Each egg is nearly half an inch long, with a hard, pearly pink shell—just like a small bird's egg.

Scientists think that Powelliphanta snails can live for up to twenty years.

Until the 1970s, the Powelliphanta snail was known as the Paryphanta snail in English, and pūpūrangi in te reo Māori. Now, scientists know that Powelliphanta and Paryphanta snails belong to different families.

E HAY
Hay, Gay,
Watch out, snail! :

_09/17

High-Flying Stars

by John Fawaz

SCHOLASTIC INC.

New York   Toronto   London   Auckland   Sydney
Mexico City   New Delhi   Hong Kong   Buenos Aires

PHOTO CREDITS

All photos are © NBA/Getty Images
Front cover: (left to right) David Liam Kyle; Noah Graham; Jesse D. Garrabrant

Interiors:
(3, 6, 21) Andrew D. Bernstein; (4, 5, 19) Noah Graham; (7, 8) Nathaniel S. Butler;
(9) David Sherman; (10) Bob Binder; (11, 27) Fernando Medina; (12) Kent Horner;
(13, 14, 15, 17, 22, 29) Jesse D. Garrabrant; (16) Layne Murdoch; (18, 20) Rocky Widner;
(23) Ronald Martinez; (24) David Liam Kyle; (25, 26) Barry Gossage; (28) Victor Baldizon;
(30) Kent Smith; (32) Joe Murphy

ISBN-13: 978-0-439-91240-2
ISBN-10: 0-439-91240-7

12 11 10 9 8 7 6 5 4 3 2 1   7 8 9 10 11/0

Printed in the U.S.A.
First printing, February 2007
Book Design: Kim Brown and Henry Ng

Carmelo Anthony
Clutch Player

Carmelo Anthony's favorite player growing up was Magic Johnson. So imagine the thrill when sportswriters liken Anthony, with his terrific all-around game, to the former Lakers' star.

"The comparisons to Magic are a huge compliment," says Anthony. "He's my favorite player."

The 6-foot 8-inch Anthony is similar in height to Johnson, and plays the game with enthusiasm and a seemingly endless smile, much like Magic. Moreover, Anthony thrives in the clutch, just like Magic. In 2005–06, Anthony gave Denver five victories with buzzer beaters.

"In my career, I don't know if I've ever had a guy make as many shots when it counts," Nuggets' coach George Karl said of Anthony.

Coming through in the clutch is nothing new to Anthony. He led Syracuse to the 2003 national title, taking apart Texas by 33 points with a dunkfest in the semifinal game and then tallying 20 points, 10 rebounds, and 7 assists against Kansas in the NCAA Championship Game. Like Magic in 1979, Anthony was named Most Outstanding Player of the NCAA Tournament.

"[Anthony] has done more for Syracuse basketball than any player we've ever recruited or that's ever played here," said Jim Boeheim, who has coached the Orange since 1976. "To lead his team to a national championship as a freshman is truly a historic moment in basketball. I'm very thankful that he was here with us."

The Nuggets were also thankful to have him. Denver selected Anthony with the third overall pick in the 2003 NBA Draft, and he made an immediate impact. The super rookie scored 21.0 points per game in 2003–04 while leading the Nuggets to their first playoff appearance since 1994–95.

Behind Anthony, Denver made its third consecutive playoff appearance in 2005–06, something the Nuggets had not done since 1990. He enjoyed his finest season yet, posting career highs in scoring average (26.5 points per game), field goal percentage (.481), and free throw percentage (.808).

"He's had a great year," Clippers' coach Mike Dunleavy said before his team played Denver in the 2006 NBA Playoffs. "His all-around game has improved. Offensively, he's got the low-post game, he's very explosive off the dribble, he's a good finisher, [and] his outside shooting is getting better all the time."

How did Anthony improve his shooting? Practice, practice, practice. By his estimate, he attempted 1,000 jump shots a day during the summer, and kept at it during the season.

"We love him," said Nuggets' guard Andre Miller. "He's doing a lot of scoring . . . and making plays for other people. Melo's mixing it up.

"He's getting to the basket, and he's comfortable making plays down the stretch. He's been big."

Anthony has them all smiling in Denver.

Kobe Bryant

Soaring Ever Higher

For Kobe Bryant, a dunk is often more than just a dunk. It's a statement.

"If someone's dominating the middle," Lakers' forward Luke Walton said, "Kobe will come over and say, 'Next time I get in the lane I'm going to dunk on that person.' And most of the time he'll make it happen."

For Bryant, a slam dunk at the right moment can turn the tide. It can stop a run by an opponent, or start one by the Lakers. It can fire up the crowd. It can send a message, telling the other team that he will not be denied.

Bryant's dunks also send a message to his Lakers teammates, telling them, "Follow me." Not that they need the hint. The Lakers' revamped roster is one of the youngest in the league. Bryant, once the kid, is now the veteran, the leader.

In 2005–06, Bryant did exactly that — he led. The Lakers' star scored 35.4 points per game, the highest scoring average in a season since Michael Jordan (37.1) in 1986–87. Bryant posted the seventh-highest point total (2,832) in NBA history.

While the inexperienced Lakers struggled to learn the team's complex offense, Bryant carried them. He has an answer for every defense: He can spin left or right, shoot fallaway jumpers, spot up for threes, fake his man into the air, elevate over anyone, and of course, the slightest opening will allow him to drive to the hoop. Trap him on a drive and Bryant will go around for a reverse layup, or he will hang in the air, for no player can stay aloft as long as he can.

Bryant scored 40 or more points 21 times, including six games with 50 or more. In December, he scored 62 points in 33 minutes against Dallas. At the end of the third quarter, when Bryant sat down for the night, he had 62 points — while the Mavericks had only 61 as a team.

That set the stage for a January 22 game against Toronto. The Lakers, struggling at home,

fell behind by 18 points to the Toronto Raptors. That's when Bryant took over, exploding for 55 points in the second half to rally Los Angeles to a 122–104 victory. Bryant's total for the night: 81 points.

His performance not only electrified the Lakers' crowd but the entire league. Despite the late hour on a Sunday night, players around the NBA were calling each other, asking the same thing: "Can you believe this?" Even Bryant was surprised.

"Not even in my dreams [could I imagine this]," he said. "This was something that just happened. It's tough to explain."

Lakers coach Phil Jackson, who coached Jordan in Chicago, said, "I've seen some remarkable games but I've never seen anything like that."

Nor had anyone else. Bryant's 81 points ranked second in NBA history, surpassed only by the legendary Wilt Chamberlain, who scored 100 points in a 1962 game. Bryant scored every way imaginable, on three-pointers and dunks, on jump shots and running one-handers. Fans around the world could not get enough of it: More than one million users downloaded the video of Bryant's 81-point game from Google Video.

"I think it's entertaining, the fact that I've been able to score points," Bryant said. "The important thing is that I've been able to do it and we've been able to win."

As the season progressed, Bryant shouldered less of the burden. Improved play from his teammates spurred the Lakers to 11 victories in their last 14 regular-season games. Los Angeles returned to the NBA Playoffs after a one-season absence and nearly stunned the favored Phoenix Suns in the first round.

"It was a good season for me individually," Bryant said. "I am more proud of what we were able to accomplish as a team, getting into the postseason."

Vince Carter

Vinsanity

Is Vince Carter the greatest dunker of them all?

"People never thought they'd see anybody jump higher or better than Jordan, or Dr. J, or Dominique," said Richard Jefferson, Carter's teammate in New Jersey. "Jordan and all those guys were some great dunkers, don't get me wrong, but you can't compare them to Vince."

Dr. Julius Erving, Dominique Wilkins, Michael Jordan — all legends. But at least one of the legends agrees that Carter is in a separate category.

"I thought it was a masterpiece," Erving said after Carter's performance at the 2000 NBA Slam Dunk championship. "He was probably more spectacular with two of those dunks than anybody who has ever dunked a basketball."

During the 2000 NBA Slam Dunk championship, Carter captivated the fans and the NBA players in attendance with his dunks, each more jaw-dropping than the last. He did five dunks that no one had ever seen before, clinching a victory in the competition with one dunk left.

As Carter prepared for his final attempt, he received a standing ovation from the sellout crowd at the Oakland Arena. He then capped the performance by taking off from the free throw line and delivering an under-the-leg, one-handed windmill dunk. Carter's finale was a tribute to Erving, who had performed a similar dunk in 1984. Vinsanity was born.

Dunking in a contest, without a defense, is one thing. But what about in games, against 7-footers? Carter is even more spectacular.

In 1999–2000, just his second NBA season, he unleashed a 360 double-pump dunk amidst a crowd of Pacers. At the 2000 Olympics in Sydney, he delivered the dunk heard round the world. In a game between USA and France, Carter intercepted a pass and drove to the basket, only to find 7-foot 2-inch French center Frederic Weis blocking his path. No problem. Carter took off a step

inside the free throw line, spread his legs in midair, and leaped over Weis. He brushed the French center's head as he threw down a thunderous dunk.

Many consider it the greatest dunk ever in a game. The French press dubbed it *Le Dunk de la Mort* — "the Dunk of Death." Other players were awestruck.

"That was probably the greatest play in basketball I've ever seen," said Jason Kidd, Carter's teammate on Team USA. "Michael Jordan hasn't done that. Nobody has done that."

How to top that? How to top what many consider the greatest dunk ever? Carter has kept at it, adding to his legacy with a remarkable array of dunks — windmills, alley-oops, up-and-unders, 360s, in-your-face, or a combination of these elements. Oh, and he can score with jumpers, three-pointers, running hooks, and the rest, but dunks are what he does best.

After playing six-plus seasons in Toronto, Carter joined the New Jersey Nets in December 2004. Those who wondered if he still had game found out pretty quickly. In a game against Miami, Carter recovered a loose ball at the three-point line. He spun the ball behind his back to free himself from a defender and drove to the hoop, where Alonzo Mourning, Miami's 6-foot 10-inch center, tried to stop him. They collided shoulder to shoulder, but Carter was unstoppable, bringing the ball over his head with his right arm and dunking on top of Mourning. Vinsanity was back.

Carter averaged 24.5 points per game in 2004–05, his highest average since 2001–02. More important, he helped the Nets rally from a slow start to make the playoffs. In 2005–06, Carter (24.2 points per game) led New Jersey to the Atlantic Division title.

"People who follow us every day know how special Vince is," Nets coach Lawrence Frank said during the 2006 NBA Playoffs. "He delivers time and again. He's a special player."

Kevin Garnett

The Volcano

Kevin Garnett stands 6-feet 11-inches tall, so of course he can dunk. But we are not talking about the rebound and putback type of slam that any big man can do.

No, KG's specialty is the more spectacular kind of dunk, the windmill, the one where he flies down the court, ball cradled in his right hand, and then he brings his right arm over his head and throws it down with authority.

In other words, the kind of dunk that brings every Timberwolves' fan to their feet. Or, if Minnesota is playing on the road, the kind of dunk that brings a hush over the crowd. They never saw it coming.

"It's like a volcano," said Garnett. "You never know when I'm going to explode."

Defending a player who stands nearly 7 feet yet handles the ball like a guard is a nightmare. Single coverage in the post allows Garnett to put up a turnaround jumper or spin around his man. Double him down there and he will kick it out to a teammate for a three.

Meanwhile, big men cannot cover him on the perimeter. If they lay back to prevent the drive, Garnett will drain the three. But if the defense comes out to chase him, then watch out, because the Timberwolves' forward will take the ball to the hoop under a full head of steam.

"I dunk so hard sometimes I can't feel my hand for a couple of plays," said Garnett. But that's nothing compared to the pain his dunks inflict on opponents.

No longer "Da Kid," Garnett completed his eleventh NBA season in 2005–06, secure in his place as one of the NBA's greatest all-around players. He scores in the paint and from the outside, dishes out assists, rebounds, plays defense, and rarely misses a game. In 2005–06, he averaged 21.8 points and 12.7 rebounds per game. It marked the eighth consecutive season he averaged 20 or more points and 10 or more rebounds per game.

"Incredible experiences, all those things," Garnett said. "But I get enjoyment out of just being here and having the opportunity to come in every night and play."

"He reminds me of how basketball should be played — with passion, hard work, and discipline," said Timberwolves vice president Kevin McHale, who was a Hall of Fame forward for the Celtics.

Off the court, Garnett is equally tireless in trying to benefit the community. His numerous charitable activities included a pledge to build twenty-four homes for victims of Hurricane Katrina. The NBA recognized his efforts by presenting him with the 2006 J. Walter Kennedy Citizenship Award.

"He's a guy who treats the twelfth man on the team like he is a starter," said guard Sam Cassell, who played two seasons with Garnett in Minnesota. "He treats everyone the same. He's a very giving person, and you can go to him for advice, anything."

For Garnett, who won the 2004 NBA MVP Award and a gold medal at the 2000 Olympics, there is only one goal left: win an NBA title. He came close in 2004 when he led the Timberwolves to the Western Conference Finals. But he has not been discouraged.

"I've always understood that everything is not always going to be good," Garnett said in the final month of the 2005–06 season. "I've always embraced the fact that there are going to be some difficult times, especially when you're dealing with change.

"I can only control what I do, so I go out and lace them up every night . . . and I go out there and give it my all."

Dwight Howard
Superstar in the Making

When the Magic selected eighteen-year-old Dwight Howard with the first pick in the 2004 NBA Draft, they saw a player with immense talent who could be a superstar in a few years. He is that rare big man (he is 6-feet 11-inches tall) who combines size with great leaping ability and agility.

Though inexperienced, Howard has progressed ahead of the Magic's schedule. He started all 82 games in 2004–05 and averaged 12.0 points and 10.0 rebounds per game to earn unanimous selection to the NBA All-Rookie First Team.

Howard bulked up during the summer, adding 25 pounds to his frame so he could not be pushed around. The added strength helped him raise his averages (15.5 points and 12.5 rebounds per game) in 2005-06. He ranked second in the NBA in rebounding, and earned an invitation to play for Team USA in summer 2006.

In the ultimate sign of respect, opponents regularly double-teamed Howard. Still, they had trouble stopping him on the offensive glass, where his rebounds of missed shots quickly turned into monster dunks.

After just two seasons, Howard already counts some of the NBA's biggest stars among his fans. Phoenix guard Steve Nash said if he were to pick one young player (other than a Suns teammate) to build a team around, it would be Howard. Other stars were equally impressed.

"He is so developed," said the Spurs' Tim Duncan. "He doesn't look like a nineteen- or twenty-year-old. He has so much promise that I am just glad that I will be out of the league when he is peaking."

"That kid is a freak of nature," said the Timberwolves' Kevin Garnett. "I was nowhere near that physically talented [at Howard's age]. I wasn't that gifted, as far as body and physical presence."

Though Howard welcomes such praise, he has yet to satisfy his toughest critic: himself.

"It's not that I'm totally unhappy, but I just feel like I could have played a lot better," Howard said in March 2006. "I could have done more than I have to help us win this season. I'm the toughest critic on myself, and I'm gonna stay on myself, so I'll never feel like I've arrived."

Orlando coach Brian Hill thinks that attitude is what will turn Howard into a superstar.

"I think it's refreshing to have a player who looks at his play and evaluates what he's not doing or not enough of," Hill said. "For him to be critical of his own game and acknowledge there is still lots of room for improvement shows you that he's headed in the right direction."

Howard's focus now is on improving his offense, his response to double teams, and his shot blocking. Considering the fact that his wingspan measures 7-feet 8-inches, he thinks he should be leading the league in blocked shots.

As for double teams, Howard is determined to make opponents pay.

"It's been tough because it's so new to me. It's something I have to get used to," he said. "Guys like Shaq [Shaquille O'Neal], Tim Duncan, and Kevin Garnett, they eventually figured it out, and that's what I'm going to do."

No doubt he will figure it out, and then, as Duncan warned, watch out.

Andre Iguodala

"It's Scary How Good He Can Be"

When Andre Iguodala entered the NBA in 2004, scouts compared him to former Bulls great Scottie Pippen because of the rookie's defense, long arms, and versatility. Now, however, he is known for something else — his super slams.

That's not to say Iguodala has let things slide at the defensive end. His first duty for the Sixers is to stop the opposing team's best scorer, and he still is expected to rebound and set up his teammates for easy baskets. But the same athleticism and wingspan that make Iguodala so good on defense also help launch him to the hoop.

Iguodala came to Philadelphia from the University of Arizona, where he earned All-Pacific 10 Conference honors for 2003–04. He had three triple-doubles for Arizona that season to become only the second Pac-10 player to record multiple triple-doubles in a season (Jason Kidd was the first).

In his first NBA season, Iguodala started all 82 games for the Sixers in 2004–05, averaging 9.0 points and 5.7 rebounds per game. He earned NBA All-Rookie First Team honors, thanks to his stellar defense and solid offensive production.

One of the highlights of Iguodala's rookie season came on March 23, 2005, when he tallied 10 points, 10 rebounds, and 10 assists in a victory over Detroit. It was the first triple-double by a Sixers' rookie in fifty years.

Iguodala started all 82 games again in 2005–06, raising his scoring average to 12.3 points per game. But for the Sixers, statistics measure only part of his contribution to the team.

"He's our best perimeter defender," Sixers' coach Maurice Cheeks said. "The reason we have so many deflections on the defensive end is because of him. He anchors our defense."

On the other end of the floor, Iguodala's acrobatic slams earned him a spot in the 2006 Sprite Rising Stars Slam Dunk. He did a variety of dunks in the contest, including a lob pass to himself that he collected mid-air, then put the ball behind his back before slamming home. He and teammate Allen Iverson combined on a dunk where Iguodala came from behind the backboard and collected Iverson's pass while airborne, and then threw it down.

"I came up with that one day during the summer," Iguodala said of his dunk with Iverson. "I was in the gym, and this guy told me I couldn't touch one side of the backboard and come to the other side and dunk the ball, and I did it."

The Sixers star advanced to the final round, where he lost by one point to the Knicks' Nate Robinson. Earlier in the NBA All-Star Weekend, Iguodala had scored 30 points (on 13 of 17 shooting) to lead the second-year players to victory in the Rookie Challenge. He displayed his improved range in that game, making four of six three-pointers.

"I've been shooting the ball well this year, so as long as I'm confident, I feel like I can make all the threes I can get," he said.

For the Sixers, Iguodala's performance at the 2006 NBA All-Star Weekend served as a preview of what they expect from their budding star. Iguodala isn't rushing it, though.

"When my time comes to be the main scorer on the team, I'll be ready for that role," Iguodala said. "Just right now, it's not."

Meanwhile, the rest of the league watches and worries.

"That kid is very skilled," said Milwaukee's general manager Larry Harris. "It's scary how good he can be."

LeBron James

King James

When asked to name his greatest dunk, LeBron James did not hesitate.

"My most memorable dunk was back in the eighth grade at Readinger Middle School, during a teachers versus students game," said James. "I threw it down hard."

Dunking in eighth grade? Well, James has always been ahead of his time. After all, when he celebrated his twenty-first birthday, he was already one of the NBA's biggest stars.

Few players have entered the league with as much attention as James. When Cleveland selected him first overall in the 2003 NBA Draft, so many great things were predicted that it seemed impossible for anyone to be that good. But in his first three seasons, James proved to be all that and more.

"That name is going to stand big," Sixers' guard Allen Iverson said at the 2005 NBA All-Star Game, in James's second season. "They'll talk about him as being one of the greatest players ever."

"I think he is absolutely unique," said Spurs' coach Gregg Popovich. "He has all the skills combined: the power, the quickness, the feel for the game. This guy's got the whole package."

"Whole package" is right. The Cavaliers run their offense through James because he is their best passer, best shooter, and best at taking it to the hoop. Not to mention quite a rebounder. He can create a shot for himself, or if he draws the defense, he can deliver a perfect pass to a teammate for an easy bucket.

For Cleveland's opponents, it is truly a frightening sight when the 6-foot 9-inch, 245-pound James comes down the court at full speed. Monster jam does not even begin to describe what he does to the hoop. Give him an opening, no matter how small, and James will take the ball to the basket.

He combines power, size, quickness, and speed into an unstoppable package, made all the more unstoppable by his improved outside shoot-

ing. If opponents pack the middle to stop James from driving, he steps up and knocks down a trey. Then there is his energy, which seems endless.

"He's a strong kid," Wizards' guard Gilbert Arenas said during the 2006 NBA Playoffs. "We tried to pressure him, get him tired, but he's just going to go past you. . . . He's a very talented kid. No wonder they call him 'King James.'"

James raised his scoring average in each of his first three seasons to a career best of 31.4 points per game in 2005–06. He finished second in the balloting for the NBA Most Valuable Player Award, an honor he no doubt will win multiple times during his career. Most important, he led the Cavaliers to their first berth in the NBA Playoffs since 1998.

In the postseason, James continued to dominate, scoring 35.7 points per game in a memorable six-game series against Washington. Cleveland won that series and then nearly upset the heavily favored Pistons in the Eastern Conference Semifinals, losing Game 7 in Detroit.

"He's a great player, a phenomenal athlete," said Detroit guard Chauncey Billups. "He does things that most guys can't do. He put his team on his back and willed himself to some great plays."

In 13 playoff games, James recorded two triple-doubles and averaged 30.8 points per game. He became the first player to average at least 30 points, 8 rebounds, and 5 assists per game in the NBA Playoffs since 1963, when the legendary Oscar Robertson did it.

Though disappointed by the loss to the Pistons, James was not discouraged. He immediately went back to work, more determined than ever to win an NBA title.

"I think I've reached a point where every part of my game needs tuning up now," James said. "I don't think I need to add any more parts. I think I just need to tune everything up and just be more complete, offensively and defensively."

TOYOTA
ONICA MINOLTA
WILSHIRE HOMES
OCKETS
1
PHOENI
22
SUNS
PHOENIX
19
SUNS
ministaff

Tracy McGrady

Finishing Fast

For Rockets guard Tracy McGrady, dunking is an art form, a way to express himself.

"You've got to have some style with your dunk. You can't be plain," McGrady said. "You've got to have some type of creativity because that's what people want to see. That's what describes your personality, the type of person you are."

In that case, T-Mac is a finisher. No matter how much energy he uses to get to the hoop, he is one of the NBA's best finishers. If he can get anywhere near the basket, McGrady finds a way to put the ball in the hole, usually with a flourish.

Sometimes he finishes after a roundabout trip to the basket, maybe going baseline for a reverse slam. Other times, T-Mac is straightforward, taking off from the free throw line and using his long arms to throw it down.

McGrady has come a long way since he entered the league as a skinny teenager in 1997 with the Toronto Raptors. Though explosive, he struggled against bigger players and was scolded by his coaches for poor habits in practice.

Things began to change for him after Butch Carter became the Raptors' coach and after some long talks with his good friend Kobe Bryant, who encouraged McGrady to practice as hard as he played. As T-Mac grew stronger and improved his outside shooting, he blossomed on the court, raising his scoring average from 7.3 points per game as a rookie to 15.4 per game in 1999–2000, his third season.

In 2000, Toronto traded McGrady to Orlando, and his career took off. He averaged 25 or more points per game in each of his five seasons with the Magic, with a high of 32.1 points in 2002–03. That season, he edged Bryant (30.0) for the scoring title, and then McGrady came back and led the

league again in 2003–04, when he averaged 28.0 points per game.

In 2004, McGrady went to Houston, to partner with the Rockets' budding star Yao Ming. The two have hit it off.

"Yao is a really funny person. I don't think a lot of people realize that," McGrady said. "He's just a great guy to be around. . . . I think there's definitely a bright future for the two [of us] and the team."

In 2004–05, McGrady averaged 25.7 points per game to lead the Rockets. In December 2004, T-Mac put together one of the greatest finishes in NBA history, scoring 13 points in the final 35 seconds. His explosion lifted Houston, which trailed 74–64 with a minute to play, to an 81–80 victory over San Antonio.

"I haven't seen anybody do something like that before," the Spurs' Devin Brown said after the game. "He was just hitting shot after shot. He was fantastic."

McGrady is no longer a skinny teenager but a polished veteran (he completed his ninth NBA season in 2005–06). Though he is still young (he turned twenty-seven in May 2006), he has already accomplished a lot. Now he is focused on one goal.

"I've won a scoring title. I've had some big individual games. I've hit some big shots that I'll always look back and remember," McGrady said. "But the way the years are rolling by . . . the only thing I'm really thinking about at this point in my career is how to get those playoff wins."

Jason Richardson

Mom Knows Best

When Jason Richardson needs advice, he calls home.

"When we lose and things are tough, she'll tell me to keep my head up," Richardson said of his mom, who worked three jobs to raise Jason and his five brothers and sisters. "And she'll remind me to dunk more. I told her I was tired of dunking. She said there's a lot of guys out there who wish they could dunk."

Most NBA players can dunk, but few (if any) can dunk like Richardson. The 6-foot 6-inch guard has the speed to outrun defenders, the leaping ability to elevate above the rim, and the body control to change direction while airborne. His exploits made him a star in his home state of Michigan, where he played for Arthur Hill High School in Saginaw and helped Michigan State win the 2000 NCAA title.

Golden State selected Richardson with the fifth overall pick in the 2001 NBA Draft. J-Rich, as he is called by his teammates, quickly established himself in pro basketball by winning the NBA Slam Dunk championship in each of his first two seasons (2002 and 2003). Richardson became the first player to repeat as NBA Slam Dunk champion since Michael Jordan in 1987 and 1988.

In the 2003 Slam Dunk championship, Richardson needed 49 points (out of 50) on his final dunk to win. He approached the basket from the side, lobbing a high bounce pass that he caught on his way up. While airborne, he put the ball between his legs to switch it from his right hand to his left, and then slammed it home over his head with his back to the basket. He seemed to hang in the air forever.

He received a perfect score of 50 from the panel of judges, which included Jordan and Dominique Wilkins, Richardson's favorite player growing up. Two years later, fans voting on NBA.com selected Richardson's dunk as the greatest in the history of the NBA Slam Dunk championship.

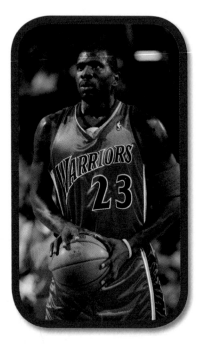

Though still an explosive dunker, Richardson has worked hard to improve the rest of his game.

"In high school, I was only known as a dunker," Richardson said. "In college, no one would guard me outside 10 feet. In the NBA, I won a dunk contest, and people thought that's all I could do. It bothers me. I take it personally. I want to be a complete player."

So Richardson got to work. He practiced every summer, attempting 1,000 jump shots a day. He improved his defense and his footwork. He worked out to increase his strength and stamina. The results have been impressive: Richardson has raised his scoring average every season, to a high of 23.2 points per game in 2005–06.

"He's developed his whole game," Wizards' guard Gilbert Arenas said. "He's a three-point threat now. He's not just a dunker anymore — he's an all-around player."

"Jason's spent a lot of time on his game, working on it, getting better," Golden State coach Mike Montgomery said. "He couldn't shoot when he got here [as a rookie]. He was a jumper and driver. Now he's a good shooter."

Of course, being a "good" shooter will never be good enough for Richardson. As soon as the season ended, he headed to the gym, for a summer of grueling workouts and 1,000 shots a day.

"I can't sit around," Richardson said at the end of the 2005–06 season. "I can't stay away from basketball. I miss it too much.

"This off-season I'm going to work on my post game, my mid-range game, and free throws. I've still got a lot to learn about the game."

Nate Robinson

Walking Tall

The shot bounced high off the rim. A crowd waited under the hoop for the rebound. Suddenly, a player soared above the forest of forwards and centers. He snared the ball with his right hand, brought it over his head, and slammed it home. The big men could only turn and wonder, "Who was that?"

That was Nate Robinson, already making a name for himself during an NBA Summer League game. When the Knicks selected Robinson in the first round of the 2005 NBA Draft, attention focused on his height. Specifically, his *lack* of height. Robinson, officially listed as 5-feet 9-inches tall, would be one of the shortest players in the NBA. Many wondered if he could play with the big boys.

Robinson answered that question resoundingly when he swooped in for his thunderous dunk. Thanks to his leaping ability, his speed, and his energy, Robinson played like someone much larger.

Knicks president Isiah Thomas made that point when he drafted Robinson. The first thing you notice about him is his height, said Thomas, but "the second thing you notice is the toughness he possesses and the confidence he has, and his talent. . . . I have no doubt if Nate was 6-1 or 6-2 he would have been the first or second pick."

Robinson attended the University of Washington, the only school that would let him play both football and basketball. He followed in the footsteps of his father, Jacque Robinson, who had been a star running back at the school.

As a freshman, Nate Robinson started six games at cornerback for the Huskies football team. As soon as football season ended, he took to the hardwood without much practice or preparation. At Santa Clara, in just his second college game, he scored 19 points in 18 minutes. Santa Clara fans gave him a standing ovation. A star was born.

"You zone in on his every move because you don't know what he's going to do next," said Washington coach Lorenzo Romar. "It might be a

big dunk or it might be a defensive play where he jumps in and steals a pass. Or maybe he takes a charge. You don't know, but you want to see."

Robinson never returned to the football field after his freshman year. He became a star for the Huskies basketball team, leading them to consecutive berths in the NCAA Tournament and earning notice from NBA scouts and players.

"As an opponent, I always hated to face players like that," Knicks' guard Quentin Richardson said. "He's going to . . . guard you over 94 feet [the length of the court], be a disrupter, a pest.

"He plays hard. He plays with heart. The [Knicks] fans will love him."

Indeed they did, right from the start. Robinson won over New York crowds with his boundless energy and enthusiasm. He seemed to be constantly in motion, going up and down like he was on a pogo stick.

He continued to deliver spectacular dunks throughout the first half of the season, riding the wave to the 2006 Sprite Rising Stars Slam Dunk championship, held during All-Star Weekend. Most rookies would have been happy just to be invited. Robinson, though, came to win — and win he did.

In so doing, Robinson became only the second player shorter than 6 feet tall to win the competition. The first was 5-foot 7-inch Spud Webb, who won in 1986. Webb, long since retired, played a supporting role in Robinson's most memorable dunk.

The Knicks' guard brought Webb out of the stands and put him in front of the basket. Robinson ran toward the hoop, received a bounce pass from Webb, and then vaulted over him and slammed it home. Robinson's dunk received a perfect score of 50 from the judges.

"It's great," Robinson said. "I can go down in history now. I'm hoping to be a legend now like Spud one day."

Josh Smith
Shock and Awe

At the 2005 NBA All-Star Weekend, Josh Smith introduced himself to the NBA.

The Hawks' rookie, competing in the NBA Slam Dunk championship, advanced through the first round, thanks to a variety of dunks. The highlight came when he soared over a seated player (Denver's Kenyon Martin) and slammed it home.

In the final round, Smith put on a Dominique Wilkins jersey, and then flew in for a windmill hammer slam, just like Wilkins used to do. Smith earned a perfect score for that dunk, and also for his final dunk, a 360-degree left-handed slam.

Wilkins marveled at Smith's performance, especially his windmill dunk.

"He shocked me with that one," said Wilkins. "That was outstanding."

Outstanding, and fitting. Smith grew up in Atlanta rooting for Wilkins, one of the most exciting players in NBA history (his nickname was the "Human Highlight Film"). The dunk competition gave Smith a chance to honor the legendary Hawks player while taking his place as Wilkins' successor.

"I kind of surprised him with that," Smith said of wearing Wilkins' jersey. "He didn't know I was going to do that, but I was going to do a dunk symbolizing what he did in previous years."

Smith's dunk announced his arrival as one of the NBA's highfliers, a remarkable 6-foot 9-inch player who could elevate to block a shot at one end, and then race down the court and elevate even higher for an earth-shattering dunk. Though officially a guard, Smith's height, vertical leap, and wingspan allowed him to play anywhere.

"He was talking about [filling my shoes] after he won [the dunk contest]," Wilkins said. "But he has his own shoes now."

Smith joined the Hawks after Atlanta selected him with the seventeenth overall pick in the 2004 NBA Draft. He had a ton of athletic ability, but he was definitely a raw talent.

"We think he has things you can't teach — the naturally athletic body, he's long and rangy, he plays above the rim — and we have to work on the skill sets that he needs," Atlanta general manager Billy Knight said on draft day. "He's been good up to this point with just athleticism."

Smith jumped right in, starting 59 games as a rookie and leading the Hawks with 1.95 blocked shots per game. In a game against Dallas, he blocked 10 shots, a remarkable feat for a forward. He averaged 9.7 points per game, with most of his points coming on dunks.

As soon as the season ended, he went to work on improving his game, especially his outside shooting. (He made just 4 of 23 three-point attempts his first season.) In 2005–06, however, he still struggled from long range, at least initially. Then suddenly the jump shots started to fall. For the season, Smith made 34 of 110 three-point shots. All 34 of his treys came after February 22.

"I worked really hard with [assistant coach] Larry Drew on it," said Smith. "I was open one time and I took it. I made it, so I kept shooting."

Smith raised his scoring average to 11.3 points per game, and finished fourth in the NBA in blocked shots (2.6 per game). He scored 17.5 points per game during the season's final 12 games. Smith, just twenty years old at season's end, seemed on the verge of stardom.

"As the years go by, he's going to be more and more effective," said Wizards' forward Antawn Jamison. "He's effective now."

Amaré Stoudemire
Center of Attention

Every basketball team runs the screen-and-roll. But thanks to Amaré Stoudemire, the Phoenix Suns have taken the most basic tactic in the game and turned it into the most effective — and spectacular — play in the NBA.

For the Suns, it begins with Stoudemire setting a screen for guard Steve Nash. As Nash dribbles by, Stoudemire reads the defense and either steps back to position himself for a 15-foot jump shot or rolls off the screen and toward the basket.

The defense, no doubt, would prefer the jump shot. After all, though Stoudemire is an excellent shooter, there is a chance he will miss. On the other hand, no defender wants to try to stop a 6-foot 10-inch, 245-pound player barreling to the hoop, especially one who attacks the rim with so much power and speed.

"He plays with a passion and force," said New Jersey coach Lawrence Frank. "He has an amazingly fast step for a guy his size."

That's why when Stoudemire rolls toward the hoop, he often has a clear path to the basket. Stoudemire receives the pass from Nash and goes up. With the ball in his right hand above his head, he takes it to the rim. In one quick motion, he slams the ball through the hoop. The crowd roars, while the defenders can only shake their heads.

When Suns' coach Mike D'Antoni moved Stoudemire from forward to center in 2004, many questioned the decision. They said bigger centers would dominate the undersize Stoudemire, who would be playing out of position. Even Stoudemire wondered if he could play in the middle.

"I was a little skeptical, knowing that most centers are 7 feet and 300 pounds," said Stoudemire.

As it turned out, opposing centers are the ones who have had trouble. Stoudemire uses his quickness and leaping ability to go over and above big men, and he is much too strong for most forwards. As a result, he is unstoppable around the hoop.

"I don't think he is out of position," D'Antoni said. "He puts everybody else out of position."

Stoudemire prepared for playing center by hitting the gym every day during the summer of 2004. He lifted weights, practiced post-up moves, and worked on his defense. He played for the U.S. Olympic team and stayed long after practice to improve his game.

"Amaré was an athletic phenomenon and a dunker when he came into the league," said San Antonio coach Gregg Popovich, an assistant on the 2004 U.S. Olympic team. "There wasn't much variety in his game. He'd go one way [to his right] and he'd be like a bull in a china shop.

"Now he goes both ways. Now he can hit the mid-range jumper. Now he runs the floor and rebounds at both ends. Amaré has put in the time. . . . That's how great players are made."

For Stoudemire, the work is never done.

"When I do work out, I work out pretty hard, and I work on every aspect of the game," Stoudemire said. "I want to reach my full potential, and I think my full potential is unlimited. So, I want to get there. I want to get there, like, *yesterday.*"

Unfortunately, a knee injury sidelined Stoudemire for all but three games in 2005–06, putting his plans on hold. But he promised to be better than ever in 2006–07.

"This year's been tough," Stoudemire said. "I had high expectations for myself this year, extremely high. I've just got to postpone it until next season."

Dwyane Wade

Flash

Heat players call Dwyane Wade "Flash," a nickname given to him by Shaquille O'Neal. The name fits — no matter where Wade is on the court, in an instant he could be at the hoop. Blink, and you might miss him.

That's because Wade is one of the fastest players in the NBA. No defender can keep up with him. On some of his drives, he disappears into the middle, only to emerge above the crowd to throw down a dunk.

Sometimes, though, the defense manages to cut him off. But that is not a problem for Wade, who simply spins away from trouble to create a shot or dish to a teammate for an easy bucket.

"He's the most dynamic player in the game right now," said Detroit coach Flip Saunders. "He can make something basically out of nothing."

In 2005–06, Wade raised his game to yet another level, thanks to his improved accuracy from long range. As he rained down jump shots, defenders could no longer clog the middle. His outside shooting opened up his inside game even more.

Wade posted career bests in scoring (27.2 points per game) and rebounding (5.7 per game) in 2005–06. He also improved on the defensive side of the ball, using his speed and quickness to average nearly two steals per game.

Wade, in just his third season, went from rising star to superstar. He was compared to Michael Jordan and Magic Johnson, among others. Though thankful for the praise, Wade remained humble.

"There's a kid inside of me who loves to play the game of basketball . . . and I'm just trying to do my best job at it," Wade said. "Those guys [Jordan and Johnson], I'm not even close to that. I've got to win a lot of championships to get there."

For Wade, the comparisons to Jordan are especially sweet, because the Bulls star was Wade's favorite player growing up in Chicago. Like Jordan, who was cut from the junior varsity team in high school, Wade was not an immediate success at basketball.

"I was small, so while I was always a step ahead of people . . . when it came to playing with players who were a little taller or older, I struggled," Wade said. "I didn't play varsity until my junior year [at Richards High School in Oak Lawn, Illinois] because I was just too small.

"But as I started growing, I was able to maintain my speed, and that's what put me over the top."

Wade made the varsity team after spending the summer before his junior year working on his ball handling and shooting. Plus, he grew several inches. He quickly emerged as the top player for Richards High, though he did not dunk the ball until his senior season.

Indeed, though Wade excelled, his game was not spectacular enough to attract the attention of college scouts. Only Marquette offered him a scholarship.

Wade continued to develop in college, winning First Team All-America honors in 2002–03. Now he had everybody's attention, especially in the NBA. Miami selected him with the fifth overall pick in the 2003 NBA Draft.

Wade became an immediate starter for the Heat, despite playing the new position of point guard (he had been a shooting guard in college). He helped Miami improve from 25–57 in 2002–03 to 42–40 in his rookie season.

Wade and the team have only gone up from there. Last June, D-Wade led the Heat to take the 2006 finals 4–2 against the Dallas Mavericks, scoring 34.6 points per game, the third highest average for a player in his first NBA Finals. Dwyane received the MVP trophy for his near record-breaking performance. He's come a long way from the days when he could not even make the team.

"He works as hard as anyone I have ever played with, if not harder," said Travis Diener, who played with Wade at Marquette. "He deserves everything he gets. He's a good teammate, he's a good friend, and I know he's a good husband and father."

Gerald Wallace

G-Force

Gerald Wallace is sometimes called "Crash" because he is fearless, a 6-foot 7-inch bundle of energy. He flies around the court, on offense and defense. He contests every shot. He soars for dunks. He is a body in motion at all times on the court.

Where does all that energy come from? Maybe from the three seasons Wallace sat on the bench in Sacramento. Wallace was talented but raw when he entered the league in 2001, and the Kings were loaded at forward. So he sat and watched — and took notes.

"I think that was a great place for him to learn, to be around great coaches and a veteran team and see how you work," said Sixers' forward Chris Webber, who was Wallace's teammate with the Kings. "He needed Sacramento, I feel, to be where he is now."

When Wallace came into the league, his dunks received all the attention. As a rookie, he finished second in the 2002 NBA Slam Dunk championship. He still brings crowds to their feet with his amazing leaps and monster jams. But those slams did not earn him any more playing time in Sacramento.

So, in 2004, Wallace asked the Kings to leave him unprotected in the expansion draft. The Charlotte Bobcats, the NBA's newest franchise, selected him.

"I just looked at it as a new organization, a new start, and a new Gerald Wallace. It was just a great opportunity for me," Wallace said.

Wallace had never been known for his defense, but he showed that his time in Sacramento had not been wasted. In his first season with the Bobcats (2004–05), he immediately established himself as a defensive stopper, finishing ninth in the NBA with 1.67 steals per game. His leaping ability, quickness, and long arms frustrated some of the league's top scorers.

"I watched him work out right before his rookie year and I remember how raw he was," said Minnesota coach Dwane Casey. "Just to see him

now, how polished of a player he is, how smart a defender he is . . . he's just come such a long way and he's the heart and soul of his team."

In 2005–06, Wallace continued to improve. He became the first NBA player since David Robinson (in 1991–92) to average more than two blocks (2.09) and more than two steals (2.51) per game in a season. He raised his scoring average to a team-high 15.2 points per game (up from 11.1 the season before) and pulled down 7.5 rebounds per game.

The increased offensive production did not come as a surprise to Wallace, who was more excited about his improvement on the other side of the ball.

"I am mostly proud of my defense," said Wallace. "I could always score, but what separates great players from average players is the guy who can do the job on both ends."

Meanwhile, Wallace's hustle made him a crowd favorite in Charlotte. The Bobcats conducted an online poll to give him a nickname, and fans selected "G-Force" because of the way he energized the team.

Wallace supplies that energy at both ends of the floor, often starting a fast break with a steal and ending it by throwing down a windmill dunk that electrifies his teammates and the crowd. When he does that, it is clear he has found a home.

"I think this has been the right place," said Wallace. "I've been improving every year and this is exactly where I want to be. It was a hard three years for me in Sacramento . . . but I learned a lot sitting and watching."

Hakim Warrick

The Helicopter

After the Memphis Grizzlies selected Hakim Warrick in the first round of the 2005 NBA Draft, he did not take long to make the highlight reel. He gave fans a thrill almost immediately.

In a preseason game against Washington, Warrick dribbled the ball about 18 feet away from the basket. He spotted an opening, and with a sudden burst he drove to the hoop. Three Wizards converged, but they could only watch helplessly as Warrick slammed home a thunderous dunk that brought the crowd and even his teammates to their feet.

"My eyes get big [when I'm left open], and I just want to attack the rim," said Warrick. "If I get a step on anybody, I think I can go up there and finish."

The 6-foot 9-inch forward plays like a 7-footer thanks to his 38-inch vertical leap and his long arms (his college teammates nicknamed him "The Helicopter"). All his skills were on display when he helped Syracuse win the 2003 national title. He had a memorable dunk against Texas in the semi-final game, and he had an even more memorable block in the championship game against Kansas, when he rejected the potential game-tying shot with 1.5 seconds left.

Two years later, Memphis chose Warrick with the nineteenth overall selection in the 2005 NBA Draft. Grizzlies' president Jerry West raved about Warrick's athleticism, his rebounding, and his work ethic.

"He has been a tremendous player in the Big East [Conference] and has gotten better every year," said West. "He's a great kid . . . and we think he is going to be a great player in the NBA."

There was no question that Warrick would make the effort. He has always been focused and willing to work to achieve his goals, on and off the court. In high school, he asked to transfer from his local school to a small, suburban high school because it offered more challenging coursework.

"It was a tough adjustment," Warrick said. "It was a small Quaker school outside Philadelphia and it was prestigious for academics. . . . I had to buckle down and really apply myself."

Despite the long commute and the extra studying, Warrick met the challenge in the classroom while continuing to shine on the court. "Skinny," the nickname he received because of his lean frame, earned a scholarship to Syracuse University.

He worked on his game relentlessly, but not at the expense of his studies. Warrick earned his degree in retail management in 3½ years. He raised his scoring average every year and became a fan favorite in Syracuse, thanks to his hustle and explosiveness. He capped his college career by averaging 21.4 points and 8.6 rebounds per game as a senior.

The NBA offered a new set of challenges. Despite his limited playing time as a rookie (11 minutes per game), Warrick showed enough brilliance to earn a spot in the 2006 NBA Slam Dunk championship. He built up his strength, forever retiring the nickname "Skinny."

For the next step, Warrick must improve his jump shot. Once that starts to fall, defenders will have to come out to cover him, which will open up the lane for him to drive and deliver more spectacular dunks.

Another challenge that he will conquer, no doubt.